Date: 11/27/19

J 590 HAR
Harrison, Paul,
Beasts and bugs /

Beasts and Bugs

WORLD
BOOK

www.worldbook.com

World Book, Inc.
180 North LaSalle Street
Suite 900
Chicago, Illinois 60601
USA

For information about other World Book publications,
visit our website at www.worldbook.com or call
1-800-WORLDBK (967-5325).

For information about sales to schools and libraries,
call 1-800-975-3250 (United States), or 1-800-837-5365
(Canada).

Library of Congress Cataloging-in-Publication Data for
this volume has been applied for.

This edition: ISBN: 978-0-7166-4062-2 (hc.)
ISBN: 978-0-7166-4056-1 (set, hc.)

Also available as: ISBN: 978-0-7166-4068-4 (e-book)

Printed in China by Shenzhen Wing King Tong Paper
Products Co., Ltd., Shenzhen, Guangdong
1st printing July 2018

Produced for World Book by
White-Thomson Publishing Ltd

www.wtpub.co.uk

Author: Paul Harrison
Editor: Izzi Howell
Design/Art director: Claire Gaukrodger
Illustrator: Rob Davis/The Art Agency

Cover artwork: © Doug Holgate

Staff

Executive Committee

President
Jim O'Rourke

Vice President and
Editor in Chief
Paul A. Kobasa

Vice President, Finance
Donald D. Keller

Vice President, Marketing
Jean Lin

Vice President, International
Sales
Maksim Rutenberg

Vice President, Technology
Jason Dole

Director, Human Resources
Bev Ecker

Editorial

Director, New Print
Tom Evans

Managing Editor
Jeff De La Rosa

Librarian
S. Thomas Richardson

Manager, Contracts &
Compliance
(Rights & Permissions)
Loranne K. Shields

Manager, Indexing Services
David Pofelski

Digital

Director, Digital Product
Development
Erika Meller

Manager, Digital Products
Jonathan Wills

Graphics and Design

Senior Art Director
Tom Evans

Senior Web Designer/Digital
Media Developer
Matt Carrington

Manufacturing/Production

Manufacturing Manager
Anne Fritzinger

Proofreader
Nathalie Strassheim

A glossary of terms appears on p. 94.

Contents

Zac Newton and friends

Zac is a junior genius and inventor of the Backspace app. The app allows Zac and his friends to take virtual trips through time and space, just by snapping a selfie.

Lucía has a sharp mind and an even sharper wit. She pretends to be too cool for school, but inside she burns to learn about science.

Quick-thinking Marcus is always ready with a joke. Although he loves to clown around, he knows more than he lets on.

Ning likes to run, jump, and play ball. She may be the youngest of the group, but nobody's going to push her around.

Zac's dog, Orbit, loves to join Zac and his friends on their adventures. He's not afraid of anything—except loud noises.

Chapter 1

Creature in the Night

Ning sipped her mug of hot chocolate. "Thanks for inviting us to your house for a sleepover, Zac," she said.

"Yeah, your mom always makes the best hot chocolate!" declared Marcus, taking another swig.

"It feels so cozy here in your kitchen," said Lucía, "especially on such a dark, foggy night." She glanced out through the glass of the back door. The yard beyond was covered in mist.

"You're all very welcome," said Zac. "Aren't they, Orbit?" he added. The dog was stretched out on the floor by Zac's feet. Orbit looked up sleepily and wagged his tail.

"I think we can call that a yes," said Marcus.

Suddenly, Orbit twitched his ears. He started to growl.

"Or maybe it's a no," said Lucía. "What's wrong, Orbit?"

The dog leaped to his feet and raced to the back door. The fur on his neck stood on end, and his mouth curled into a snarl. He began to bark.

Zac put down his mug and joined Orbit at the door. "What is it, boy?" He wiped some moisture from the fogged up window to get a clearer view of the yard. Then, he gasped. "Hey, I think there's something out there... I can see it moving."

"It's probably just a cat," said Marcus. "I hope it's just a cat."

"Maybe we should go and check it out," suggested Ning.

Zac found a flashlight in a drawer. Holding Orbit firmly by the collar, he opened the door and stepped out into the night. The others followed close behind. Zac switched on the flashlight. He pointed it toward the corner of the yard, where he'd seen the strange intruder.

"There it is!" breathed Lucía, peering through the mist.

"It looks big," whispered Ning.

"Where? I can't see it!" cried Marcus.

"Over there," hissed Zac. He pointed to a shadowy

figure moving slowly through the flowers and shrubs. "It looks like some kind of wild animal—too big to be a cat."

Orbit barked, and the shape froze. For a moment, a pair of startled eyes shone back at them, reflecting the glow from Zac's flashlight. Then, with a loud clatter, the mystery creature climbed over the fence and was gone.

"Whoa, it moved quickly!" said Marcus.

"What was it?" wondered Ning.

"No idea," said Zac. "We can hunt for clues tomorrow, in the daylight."

Early the next morning, the friends went out to examine the corner of the yard where they had seen the creature. There were a few trampled plants and some scratches on the fence, but not much more to see.

"Not even a footprint," sighed Ning.

"Or a piece of dung," said Marcus.

Lucía wrinkled her nose at him.

"What?" cried Marcus. "People who track animals are always on the lookout for dung. Right, Zac?"

Zac nodded. "It's true, animal droppings, or dung, are very useful for identifying an unknown creature."

"Still, do we have to talk about dung just before breakfast?" complained Lucía.

As if on cue, Zac's dad called them in to eat.

"What are your plans for today, kids?" he asked, as they ate their breakfast of pancakes and eggs.

"I thought maybe we could just chill here," said Marcus.

"Or go skating," suggested Ning.

"Or catch a movie," said Lucía.

"Hey, look at this," said Zac, picking up the morning newspaper. He pointed at the headline: Mystery Beast Stalks Neighborhood.

Zac read the article aloud. "A number of local residents have reported sightings of an unidentified night-time visitor in their back yards. The beast has been seen in the area of Park Street, Forest Lane, and Lake Avenue. Witnesses have described it as looking like a cougar, a coyote, or a large raccoon…"

"How can the same animal look like a cougar, a coyote, and a raccoon?" frowned Lucía. "People around here should get their eyes checked."

"To be fair, the nights have been pretty foggy lately," said Zac's dad.

"I'm sure it's just a stray cat," said Marcus hopefully. "On foggy nights, cats can look pretty creepy."

"Hey, wouldn't it be cool if we solved the mystery and found this creature?" said Zac.

"Great idea!" said Ning. "Let's do it."

"Just be careful," Zac's dad warned. "You know it can be dangerous to approach a wild animal. So be sure to keep your distance if you find anything."

After breakfast, the children prepared to search the neighborhood. They packed snacks and plenty of water. Zac pulled up a map of the area on his phone, and Zac's dad lent them a guidebook to local wildlife.

"Maybe we should also bring along some cat food," suggested Marcus.

"For the last time, Marcus, it's not a cat!" Lucía groaned.

"Marcus has a point, though," said Zac. "Some kind of bait might come in handy. Let's take some of Orbit's food. You don't mind, do you, boy?"

Orbit whined as Zac took three cans from the cupboard and put them into his backpack.

"Where do we start?" wondered Ning.

"How about the forest preserve?" suggested Zac. He showed them a green area on the map. "It's close to all the streets where the creature's been spotted, including this one."

"Yeah, maybe the creature rests there during the day, then goes looking for food in people's back yards at night," said Lucía.

The children set out for the forest preserve. They spent the whole day there, hiking the trails and searching for signs of the mystery beast.

The closer they looked, the more clues they found that had been left behind by animals. They found goose footprints at the muddy edge of a pond and half-nibbled nutshells left by squirrels. There were slime trails made by slugs and even a pile of bird feathers, where a fox may have snatched a meal.

None of these animals—except maybe the fox— seemed likely to be their mystery beast, though.

"Maybe we should try luring the beast out into the open, so we can get a look at it," suggested Marcus.

They placed a dish of dog food in a clearing to see if they could tempt the beast from its hiding place. The children took cover behind some trees and waited.

Eventually, a crow fluttered down to peck at the dog food. Orbit quickly chased it away.

After that failure, they were about to give up hope. Then Ning shouted, "Hey, come and look at this!" She crouched over a small patch of muddy ground.

The others gathered around. Ning was staring at a mark in the mud.

"What is it?" asked Marcus.

"A footprint," said Ning.

"Are you sure?" asked Lucía, squinting at it from

different angles.

Ning traced the shape with her finger. "Look, here's the main part of the foot, and these are the five toe marks."

"That's not like any footprint I've ever seen," said Marcus. "It almost looks like a handprint. And why is that toe so far away from the other ones?"

Flipping through his guidebook, Zac muttered, "There's nothing like it in this book. Maybe you've found our mystery beast, Ning."

"Or maybe you've found a few random marks in the mud," suggested Lucía.

"I'll take a picture anyway," said Ning, snapping the image with her phone.

Chapter 2

The Prehistoric Sea

The children began to make their way back to Zac's house. "It's amazing, when you think about it," said Marcus.

"What's amazing?" asked Lucía.

Marcus explained. "We saw, or nearly saw, so many animals today: crows, squirrels, frogs, foxes, beetles, slugs, spiders, and whatever made that footprint... They're all so different. And, that's just here in our own little forest preserve. When you think about how many different animals there are in the whole wide world, it blows your mind! It makes you wonder how the world got to be so full of different animals."

"I'm guessing there must have been a time when there were fewer kinds of living things," said Ning, "and then more and more kinds of living things came along. Right, Zac?"

Zac nodded. "There is one particular time I can

think of when animal life really got going. All kinds of new animals started appearing…" He trailed off as an idea struck him. "Hey, maybe we could go back there." He pulled out his phone and clicked on one of the icons.

"The Backspace app!" cried Lucía in excitement.

The Backspace app was Zac's most amazing invention. It allowed them to go on a virtual visit to any time or place in history, all without leaving the present.

"You remember how it works?" asked Zac.

The friends gathered around him. He stretched out his arm with the phone in his hand, as if taking a selfie. "Make sure you can see yourselves on the screen," Zac said. "We don't want to leave anyone behind!"

They all hugged in a bit closer, and Zac pressed the button.

FLASH!

ZUMMMMMMmmmmmmmm…

When the flash faded, the scene around them had changed. The forest preserve was gone. The children found themselves bobbing a few feet above the ocean floor. Strange creatures crawled along in the mud below. There were worms covered in spikes and flat, roundish animals with flexible shells. A beautiful jellyfish, shaped like a lantern, drifted past them. None of these creatures looked familiar.

Zac suddenly noticed the other children holding their breath. Lucía's face was turning purple.

"It's okay," Zac said. "Remember, it's just virtual reality. In reality, we're all still back in the forest preserve. You should be able to breathe normally."

Marcus let out an explosive puff of air. A stream of virtual bubbles rose from his mouth.

"Where are we?" gasped Ning.

"*When* are we?" Lucía added.

"I've brought you to a time called the Cambrian Period, around 540 million years ago," said Zac. "We're underwater, because it is unclear if there was any life outside the sea yet."

"Wait… did you just say 540 *million* years ago?" gulped Marcus. "That's farther back than the dinosaurs!"

"Way farther," said Zac. "You were wondering how life on Earth developed such variety. Well, the answer is evolution. Evolution is how living things change over many generations. Eventually, they can even become a new species, or kind of living thing. Evolution can work pretty slowly, so we have to travel a long way back to see big changes."

"But why the Cambrian Period, exactly?" said Ning.

"The Cambrian Period was a really important time in the history of life," Zac explained. "For billions of years before, living things were pretty simple—bacteria and algae and stuff like that. But in the Cambrian Period, lots of more complicated creatures started to appear. As you can see, they developed an amazing variety of body structures—stuff that living things had never had before. Some people call this great leap in diversity the Cambrian explosion, because it all happened over only 25 million years."

"Only 25 million years?!" chuckled Marcus.

"That's fast by evolutionary standards, believe me!" said Zac.

"So why did living things change so suddenly?" asked Ning.

"Scientists aren't sure, but it might have had something to do with rising oxygen levels. Animals use oxygen to make energy. All that extra oxygen could have led to some interesting changes," Zac explained.

"Some scientists think that the changes in animal

life began even earlier, but that earlier animals didn't leave behind many fossils. Fossils are the remains of living things preserved in rock. Studying fossils is how we learn what life was like in Earth's past!"

A wormlike creature wriggled through the dirt below them, stirring up clouds of mud.

"In any case," Zac said, "all the animals in our time—their story started here. These creatures are like their great-great-super-great grandparents."

"Are you sure?" said Ning. "Besides that jellyfish, none of these animals looks familiar to me."

Zac pointed to a flat beast with a hard, jointed shell crawling across the sea floor. "See that? That's a trilobite. It's a kind of arthropod, an relative of today's insects, spiders, and crustaceans. And that creature with the shell and the long, fleshy thing that looks like tongue—that's a lingula, a relative of the modern clam."

"What about our ancestor?" asked Marcus.

"Did any of these critters evolve into us?"

Zac scanned the waters until he saw a tiny eel-like creature swimming among seaweed. "That little animal over there is called a *chordate*," he said. "It has the beginnings of a backbone, which makes it the ancestor of all vertebrates. Vertebrates are animals with backbones. That includes fish, birds, reptiles, amphibians, and mammals... including humans."

"Hey, little fella," Marcus cooed at it. "Live long and prosper. And try not to get eaten."

Suddenly, a shrimplike monster nearly as big as Orbit swam up. It swallowed the chordate whole.

"Oh, no!" cried Marcus. "There goes humanity, civilization, comics... baseball!"

"Don't worry, plenty of other chordates survived!" chuckled Zac.

"What is that thing?" wondered Ning, as the shrimp-thing swam closer.

"*Anomalocaris,*" said Zac. "It was a major predator of the Cambrian seas."

The creature's sides were crowded with paddlelike fins that rippled as it swam. Its bulging eyes seemed to scan them curiously.

"Are you sure we're safe here?" gulped Marcus.

"I'd rather not wait around to find out," said Zac. He pressed a button on his phone. The virtual sea disappeared, and they found themselves back in the forest preserve.

Chapter 3

An Idea with Legs

"I have a question," said Ning, as the children made their way out of the forest preserve. "You know what you were saying just now, Zac, about mammals, birds, fish, and reptiles? Why do we divide animals into groups like that? Why not just group them by how they move? We could have the fliers and the swimmers. Then we could have the crawlers, the runners, and the hoppers."

"Or, we could classify animals by their habitat, the kind of place where they live," proposed Lucía. "We'd have forest animals, sea animals, desert animals, rain forest animals, and so on."

"Or…" said Marcus, not wanting to be left out, "we could, uh… we could classify them by how many legs they have. There'd be two-leggers, four-leggers, six-leggers, eight-leggers, and so on."

"And where would snakes fit into your system, Marcus?" giggled Lucía.

"They'd be no-leggers." Marcus smiled, pleased with himself.

They turned to Zac, who was considering their suggestions. "Each of you is onto something," he said. "We could group, or classify, animals in any of those ways. In fact, people throughout history have wondered how best to classify living things. One of the first to try was an ancient Greek thinker named Aristotle. We could go and meet him, if you want…"

"Ancient Greece sounds a lot less dangerous than the Cambrian sea. Count me in," said Marcus.

They gathered around Zac's phone.

FLASH!

ZUMMMMMMmmmmmmmm…

This time, the children found themselves on a sandy, sun-baked beach. Seated on a nearby rock was a bearded man in loose clothing. In his hand was a net. He was swishing it through a pool of water, as if trying to catch something.

As the children walked toward him, he looked up and smiled in welcome.

"Excuse me, sir, are you Aristotle?" asked Zac.

"I am, indeed," the man said, putting down his net.

"We were hoping to ask you for your thoughts on how to classify animals," said Ning.

"We were wondering how you divide them into different groups," added Lucía.

Aristotle's eyes brightened. "An excellent question!" he exclaimed. "It so happens that I have been thinking about this for many years. My original system was quite simple. I divided animals by how they moved—walking, flying, or swimming."

Ning beamed with pride. "You see?" she said to the others. "Even Aristotle agrees with me."

"Well, not entirely, my dear," Aristotle continued. "The more I thought about it, the more problems

I saw in that system. A frog, for example, can both swim and walk. As for a duck, it can swim, walk, and fly."

Ning looked a little disappointed.

"So what system did you come up with next?" asked Zac.

"Counting the legs?" said Marcus hopefully.

"Actually, I started thinking about blood," said Aristotle.

"Blood?" Marcus winced.

Aristotle swished his net through the pool and caught a crab. He held it up for them to see.

"This little animal has no blood," he said. "Instead, his body holds another type of fluid. The same is true of other animals I have studied, including spiders, beetles, and snails. The fluid inside them is often clear, or sometimes it's yellow, green, or blue. But it's not red, like blood. So, I would first make a distinction between these bloodless animals and animals with blood, such as humans, dogs, birds, fish, and lizards."

Zac whispered to the others, "This is not that different from the way modern scientists divide animals into vertebrates, which have backbones, and invertebrates, which do not. Vertebrates have blood. Invertebrates have a different kind of fluid, called hemolymph."

Aristotle continued, "The animals that have blood can be further divided into four-legged, warm-blooded animals that give birth to live young."

"Mammals, in other words," Zac whispered.

"Hey, he just mentioned legs!" said Marcus excitedly.

"Birds also have blood, of course," added Aristotle, "but they lay eggs and have two legs, so they would form a separate category. Then you have animals with blood that lay eggs but have four legs, such as lizards and frogs. And, animals with blood that lay eggs but have no legs, like snakes and fish. And so on."

"Thank you, sir!" said Zac. "You've been most helpful." With the touch of a button, he whisked the children away from ancient Greece.

"Aristotle sure talks a lot, but I think we got the picture, don't you?" said Zac.

Marcus couldn't hold in his excitement. "Didn't I tell you legs were important!" He looked around, and his smile faded. "Hey, where are we? Where's the forest preserve?"

They had arrived in a snowy landscape dotted with tall fir trees.

"This is Lapland, in northern Sweden, in 1732," explained Zac. "It's the scene of the next big development in classification."

They heard a tinkling of bells. A sleigh came into sight, pulled by a reindeer. A young man dressed in furs was sitting inside. He pulled to a stop as he came near them.

"Greetings!" he cried. "I didn't expect to find people out here. Who are you?"

"We're looking for the famous Swedish scientist Carolus Linnaeus," said Zac, pronouncing the name *lih NEE uhs.*

The young man laughed. "I'm not sure about the famous part, but I am Linnaeus. How can I help you?"

"Is it true that you're developing a new way of classifying animals?" asked Zac.

"Plants and animals, yes," said Linnaeus. "This is the reason for my expedition here to Lapland. I've traveled all the way from my home city of Uppsala to investigate the plants of Lapland. I plan to publish a book on the subject, so I can try out my brand new system of classification."

"Why do you think we need a new system?" asked Ning.

"Good question, young lady," said Linnaeus.

"For almost 2,000 years, people have been using Aristotle's system. It's a good system in many ways, but I think it's now a bit out of date. Perhaps I can show you mine..."

Linnaeus reached inside a canvas bag and pulled out a large book bound in leather. He flipped through pages covered with notes and sketches of plants and animals until he came to a blank page. He reached inside his bag for a pencil and began to draw a diagram.

"First, I divide the animal kingdom into six groups called classes: birds, fish, mammals, insects, worms, and amphibians. These are based on shared characteristics. So mammals, for example, are warm-blooded. They have hair or fur. They give birth to live young, and the mothers feed their young with milk."

"That doesn't sound so different from Aristotle's system," said Marcus.

"So far, it is similar, I agree," said Linnaeus. "But,

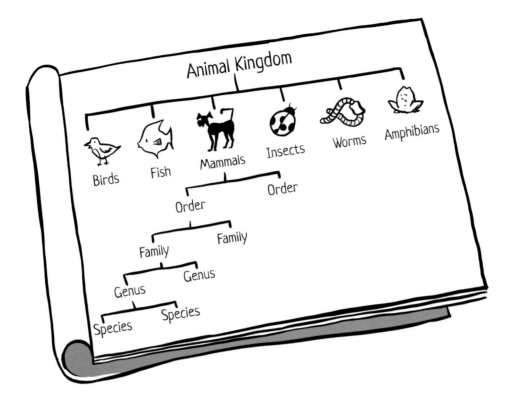

I've added many finer layers of division beneath this."

As he spoke, Linnaeus continued to add to his diagram. "So, each class is subdivided into orders, and these are further split into families. Each family is made up of genera—singular, genus—which are, finally, made up of individual species."

"Why do you need so many layers?" asked Ning.

"Because life is complex and diverse," replied Linnaeus. "Take my reindeer, for example. We can tell the furry fellow belongs to the mammal class. But there is much more to him than that. He has features that he shares with other, related animals. Look at his feet, for example. What kind of feet does he have?"

"Hoofs," said Lucía.

"Precisely!" smiled Linnaeus. "And animals with hooves are called *ungulates.*"

Linnaeus got out of his sleigh and went to kneel by the reindeer. "Now, look at how he is standing. See how the weight of his hoof is spread evenly across his third and fourth toe."

The children bent closer and saw what Linnaeus meant.

"That's why we call reindeer *even-toed* ungulates. Or, to use the Latin word, Artiodactyla. That is the name of their order. Other Artiodactyla include pigs, camels, sheep, and cows. Within that order, reindeer belong to the family Cervidae, which includes all the many kinds of deer. And within Cervidae, their genus is *Rangifer.* Their species, which happens to be the only species of *Rangifer,* is *Rangifer tarandus.*"

Linnaeus got up and dusted the snow from his breeches. "So, that is my system, and you can apply it to every single animal in the world."

"It's brilliant!" said Zac. "I'm sure they'll still be using it, or something very similar, 300 years from now."

"Very impressive," agreed Marcus. "But I think you could have done more with legs."

"Legs?" Linnaeus looked confused.

"The number of legs an animal has," Marcus explained. "You could have used that somewhere in your system."

"Thank you very much for your time, Mr. Linnaeus," said Zac hastily. "But we have to get going."

He hit the return button, and in a flash, they were back in the forest preserve.

Chapter 4
Invader

The following morning, the children met back at Zac's house to continue their investigation. Ning was the last to arrive. She looked worried.

"What is it, Ning?" asked Lucía.

"I checked the local news website this morning to see if there was any more information about the mystery beast," she said.

"Well, is there?" asked Zac.

"There were more reports last night," Ning told them. She pulled out her phone and read off the screen. "Mrs. Li of Park Street says the beast terrified her cat. Mr. Turner of Forest Lane saw it turning over his garbage can and rooting around for food scraps. And Miss Sanchez of Lake Avenue claims she saw the beast stealing from her vegetable patch. There's still no agreement on what it is, but everyone agrees it's a problem!"

"That doesn't really help us," said Lucía glumly.

"In one way it does," said Zac.

"How so?" asked Lucía.

"Well," said Zac, "it's obvious from these stories that it's an invader—a creature from somewhere else that doesn't belong here."

"Or, it could just be a pet cat that got tired of playing nice," suggested Marcus.

"It could be," said Zac, "but all the signs point to it being an invader." He was about to go on, but then he stopped as a thought struck him. "I know someone who can explain all this a lot better than I can," he said. "Are you all ready for another trip?"

"You bet!" said Marcus. "Do I need to pack sunscreen or a winter coat this time?"

"It's all virtual, silly!" said Lucía.

"Gather up, everyone!" said Zac, holding out his phone.

FLASH!

ZUMMMMMMmmmmmmm...

"Hey, we're back in the woods," said Marcus, gazing at the tall trees around them.

"This isn't the forest preserve," said Zac. "This is Wytham Woods, in Oxfordshire, England, and it's 1958—April or May, I'd guess from those bluebells." He pointed out a carpet of violet-blue flowers growing between the trees.

Just then, Orbit caught sight of a squirrel. He was about to go chasing after it when Zac pulled him back. "Virtual squirrels are even harder to catch than real ones, Orbit," Zac said, patting him on the head.

Standing in the middle of the bluebells was an older man in a tweed jacket. He was facing away from them, peering through a pair of binoculars at something high up among the branches. Zac followed the man's gaze to a nest where a bird was feeding her chicks.

"That's a common redstart, isn't it?" Zac called.

The man lowered his binoculars and turned to face the newcomers. "Indeed it is," he smiled. "You really know your birds. We're fortunate to have a thriving population of redstarts here in Wytham."

"Are you the zoologist Charles Elton?" Zac asked.

"I am," the man answered. "And you are?"

"A group of friends with a problem," replied Zac. "We're hoping you might be able to help. You see, there has been a series of disturbances in our neighborhood. People are talking about a mystery beast. The pets are frightened, garbage has been strewn all over the place, and vegetable patches have been dug up. Do you have any idea what might be going on?"

Elton rubbed his chin thoughtfully. "Have you children ever heard of something called an ecosystem?"

"Is that like a machine for recording echoes?" guessed Marcus.

"No, nothing like that!" laughed Elton. "An ecosystem is a community of living things, along with all the ways they work with one another and with their environment. This wood, for example, is an ecosystem. The birds, the insects, the squirrels, the trees, the flowers, they're all part of it. They each play their role."

"Play their role?" asked Ning. "You mean like eating one another?"

"That's one role," nodded Elton. "One animal might be a grub, which provides a tasty snack for that family of redstarts up there. But there are many other roles to perform. Another member of the ecosystem could be a butterfly, pollinating a flower so that the flower can make seeds to grow new flowers. Or an oak tree might provide acorns for the squirrels to eat. All the living things in this wood depend on one another. They also depend on nonliving things, such as water, nutrients, and sunlight. These things are part of the ecosystem, too."

"It's like a big web of connections among all the different pieces," said Lucía.

"But what does this have to do with the mystery beast?" asked Marcus.

"I'm coming to that," said Elton. "You see, an ecosystem can be quite a fragile thing. A healthy ecosystem exists in a delicate balance. If an invader arrives, it can upset that balance. Your mystery beast has invaded the ecosystem of your neighborhood, and it has unbalanced things. That's why there's so much trouble right now."

"I never thought of our neighborhood like that before," said Ning. "It makes sense, though!"

Elton continued. "If I can pass on one piece of advice, it's this—don't blame the mystery beast for any of this. It's just trying its best to survive in an unfamiliar place. This experience is probably just as upsetting for the beast as it is for you and your neighbors—maybe more so. So, track it down and capture it, if you can, but show compassion. Try to restore it to its own ecosystem. That way, everything will be in balance again."

"That's great advice, sir," said Zac. "Thank you! We'll be going now."

Chapter 5
A Glowing Discovery

"Okay," said Marcus, back at Zac's house. "I accept that the mystery beast is probably not a cat."

"At last!" cried Lucía.

"And," he continued, "I'm prepared to admit that it's not a local animal either—at least not one we know about. But, I still don't believe that it's an invader."

"If it's not local, and it's not an invader, then what is it, Marcus?" demanded Ning.

Marcus lowered his eyelids and smiled, ready to unleash a brilliant theory. "I believe what we're dealing with here is a completely new type of animal."

"Now I've heard everything," groaned Lucía.

"Think about it," Marcus continued. "That strange

footprint that Ning found, the fact that no one can agree what the animal is—it all points to this being a new species."

Ning laughed. "Are you saying it just popped into existence out of thin air?"

"No, I'm not saying that," said Marcus. "What I'm saying is that this creature is new to science. No one's ever seen it until now."

"Please, tell him he's talking nonsense, Zac," begged Lucía.

Zac frowned. He didn't like to give up on an idea right away, no matter how wacky it sounded. "Well," he thought aloud, "it's true that new species are being discovered all the time, so Marcus's theory isn't completely ridiculous. However, newly discovered animals are usually small. And, they're usually found in parts of the world that haven't been explored much, such as the deep rain forest. The idea that a large animal could live so close to humans without being discovered is pretty unlikely, to be honest."

"But it's possible, right?" said Marcus. "You just said so."

"Well…" Zac hesitated.

"Wait, Zac," Ning broke in, "did you just say new species are being discovered all the time?"

Zac nodded.

"How cool is that!" she cried. "Who discovers them?"

"Wildlife scientists, mostly." Zac smiled at her excitement. "Would you like to join one of them on an expedition—virtually, I mean!"

"Would I?" Ning whooped. "You bet!"

"Me, too," said Lucía.

"And me!" said Marcus.

"Woof!" said Orbit.

"Then gather around," said Zac, taking out his phone.

FLASH!

ZUMMMMMMmmmmmmmm...

A few seconds later, they were standing in a forest. It had trees, just like their local forest preserve. But besides that, the two places seemed totally different. Here, the plants and trees grew thickly around them. It also felt much warmer and damper than the forest preserve. Huge leaves dripped with moisture. Thick vines dangled in great loops from the branches, covered in moss. The sounds were different, too. The air was filled with the squawks of birds and the cries of monkeys.

"Where are we?" asked Lucía.

"We're in South America," said Zac, "in a rain forest in Ecuador, on the eastern slopes of the Andes Mountains. It's an area with a lot of animal life. And, much of it hasn't been discovered yet."

A few rays of sunlight poked through the canopy of leaves above their heads. Most of the forest was in shadow. Ning peered into the gloom. She thought she'd seen something move.

"What's that?" she asked, pointing toward a figure crouching in the darkness.

Orbit growled nervously.

"Could be an undiscovered species." Marcus shuddered.

"It's a wildlife scientist," said Zac. "We should go and meet her. Come on!"

The scientist was kneeling by a tree root, staring at something crawling slowly along it. Suddenly, she noticed she was being watched by four children and a dog. She jumped up, startled.

"What a surprise!" she said. "I didn't expect to find any other humans around here." She looked more like an adventurer than a scientist in a lab coat. Despite the heat, she wore long pants and boots to protect her legs. Her hair was pulled back in a headband. Her long-sleeved shirt was damp with sweat.

"Do you discover new species?" asked Ning, wide-eyed.

The scientist laughed. "Well, I suppose that's part of what I do. I'm an entomologist, a scientist who studies insects. I'm on an expedition to study the local insect life."

"Pleased to meet you!" beamed Ning. "My name's Ning, and I'm fascinated by new species."

"What is that creature you're looking at?" asked Lucía, staring at the insect on the tree root. It was a large and beautiful beetle with a long, golden brown body. On its back were two green spots. They glowed brightly in the dim forest light.

"This is a type of beetle from the genus *Pyrophorus,* which comes from a Latin word meaning *carrying fire,*" said the wildlife scientist. "You can see why it got its name, can't you? It really glows in the dark."

"Like a lightning bug," said Marcus.

The scientist glanced up at Ning. "If you're interested in new species, you've arrived at just the right moment. This is a type of *Pyrophorus* beetle I've never seen before. I know these insects pretty well—I've been studying them for 12 years—and I believe this is a new species."

Ning crouched closer to the beetle, inspecting every detail. "It gives me goosebumps just thinking about it," she murmured.

"I know exactly what you mean," said the wildlife scientist. "I feel the same way."

"So what happens now?" asked Zac. "Do you get to name it?"

"Yes," said the wildlife scientist. "And, I have to write a scientific paper describing it in detail. The paper will have to be published—shared with others who want to read it—and reviewed by other entomologists." She smiled at the beetle. "You, little fellow, are going to be a lot of hard work for me!"

"What are you going to name it?" asked Marcus.

"Well, the first part of the name must be *Pyrophorus*," explained the wildlife scientist. "That's the genus. The second part—the species name—is up to me. It'll have to be a Latin word, or something that sounds like Latin. But before I can name it, I have to prove that it really is a new species. It could just be a unique individual—the result of a mutation."

"What's a mutation?" asked Lucía.

Marcus opened his mouth to answer this. He knew all about mutation from his superhero comics. But then he stopped. He could feel something climbing up his back. It really tickled! He reached around to try and brush it off...

The wildlife scientist explained, "Sometimes, living things are born a little different from others of their species. This has to do with their genes. Living things inherit genes from their parents. Genes help determine a living thing's traits, or characteristics. Sometimes, genes get damaged, or they don't get copied properly. We call that mutation. It can result in one individual being a little different from other members of its species."

Marcus reached back as far as he could, but he still couldn't reach the thing crawling up his back. It was almost up to his neck...

"So, you're saying this could be a species that's already known about, but this individual just looks different because of a mutation," said Lucía.

"It's possible," said the wildlife scientist. "But, if I can find another example of the same beetle, that will help prove it really is a new species."

"Gotcha!" shouted Marcus, flicking at the thing on his neck. When he brought back his hand, he was startled to find a creature still clinging to his finger.

The wildlife scientist gasped. "Oh, look what you've found!"

They all stared at the beetle dangling from the tip of Marcus's finger. It looked nearly identical to the other beetle.

Gently, the scientist took the beetle from Marcus's finger and examined it more closely. "This is just what I was looking for," she said, "another individual of the same species. And this one appears to be a female." She raised her eyes to Marcus with an expression of deep gratitude. "What's your name, young man?"

"M-Marcus," he stammered.

"Marcus," said the wildlife scientist, "in your honor, I name this species *Pyrophorus marcusi.*"

Chapter 6
Finch Food

Back at Zac's house, Marcus was still buzzing with excitement. "A new species named after me! How about that? I'm going down in history!"

"Virtual history," corrected Lucía.

"The point we've learned is that there are new species out there," said Zac, "but they're usually found in out-of-the-way places."

"So where does that leave us with our mystery beast?" asked Ning. "We still don't know what it is or where it came from."

"Maybe it just evolved," said Marcus.

The others turned toward him, bewildered. "Evolved, Marcus?" asked Zac.

"Yeah!" said Marcus, with growing confidence. "The mystery beast must be a newly evolved animal.

It's the only theory that makes any sense. It's like that little chordate we saw in the prehistoric sea, which eventually evolved into us. Our mystery beast is an animal that was something else—a harmless little opossum, say. And one day, it evolved into a creature that frightens pets and digs up carrots."

"Marcus, I've never heard such…" Lucía began.

"I think," Zac interrupted, "that Marcus has brought up a good point. We've talked about evolution, but we haven't yet learned how it actually works. And, I think I know just the person to explain it."

"Are we, by any chance, about to go on another Backspace trip?" wondered Ning.

"I definitely get that feeling," said Lucía.

"Let me see your faces," said Zac, holding up his phone.

"Make room for me," said Marcus. He pushed into the frame just as Zac pressed the button.

FLASH!

ZUMMMMMMmmmmmmm...

The children found themselves on a gravel path. To the left was an oak wood. To the right, a hedge overlooked a valley. Coming down the path was a balding man with a round face and bushy sideburns. He plodded along with his head down and his hands clasped behind his back, hardly aware of his surroundings. He seemed to be deep in thought.

"This is 1846," said Zac. "We're on the grounds of Down House, in the county of Kent, England. The man coming toward us is Charles Darwin."

"Darwin!" cried Ning. "I've heard of him!"

"Did someone mention my name?" said Darwin, looking up in surprise.

Ning covered her mouth, embarrassed. "I'm sorry, sir. I was surprised to see you."

"Not as surprised as I am to see you," he said, surveying the young strangers before him. "I don't usually meet anyone here on my 'thinking path.' This is private land, you know."

"We're very sorry, sir," said Zac. "And, I promise we won't take up too much of your time, but we'd really like to hear you explain your theory of evolution."

Darwin's eyebrows shot up. "How do you know about my theory?" he spluttered. "I've been so careful to keep it secret..."

"We won't tell anyone, sir," Zac promised.

Darwin nodded. "You'd better not. I'm writing a book about it. It's going to surprise a lot of people when it comes out." He glared at each of them in turn. "But, only if no one talks about it first!"

"We understand, Mr. Darwin," said Zac.

"Good," said Darwin. "So what do you know so far?"

"We know that animals change over time," said Ning.

"We just don't know how it happens, or why," said Lucía.

Darwin nodded. "This question has interested me for a decade or more," he said, "ever since my voyage on a ship called the *Beagle*. During that trip, I spent some time on the Galápagos, a faraway group of islands in the Pacific Ocean. I observed that animals of the same type varied from island to island,

and that each variation seemed well suited to the island on which the animal lived."

"What exactly do you mean?" asked Ning.

"Well, take finches, for example," said Darwin. "There are over a dozen species of finch on the Galápagos, and they live alone on different islands. The species are almost identical—except for their beaks, which vary in shape and size. This, I later came to realize, was because of the food they eat. Depending on which island they lived, they might eat seeds, insects, grubs, leaves, cactuses, or buds and fruit. There are different kinds of food on each island, you see. And in each case, the finches' beaks were adapted to eat that particular food. Here, let me show you."

Darwin pulled a sheet of paper from inside his jacket and unfolded it before them. It was covered in sketches of the heads of various finches with different shaped beaks. "What does this tell you?" he asked the children.

Leaves

Seeds

Buds/Fruit

Insects

Grubs

Cacti

"That evolution can make animals better adapted
to their particular environment?" said Lucía.

"Exactly!" said Darwin. "And how does it do that?"

"Maybe the kid finches see their parents struggle
to eat some seeds or whatever, so they grow a better
beak for seed-eating?" suggested Marcus.

"If only it were that simple," chuckled Darwin.
"Sadly, finches do not have the power to change
the shape of their own beaks. What they do have, in

common with all other animals, is the instinct to survive and have young. This is the first point to remember: all living things are driven to survive and have young. The second point to remember is that not all young are the same. There is always variety."

"Is that because of mutation?" asked Ning, recalling what they'd learned from the wildlife scientist.

"Yes, sometimes it is!" said Darwin. "Some of those baby finches are going to be born with differently shaped beaks. Now, let's imagine we're on the island where there are lots of cactuses. On that island, some finches might, by chance mutation, be born with beaks that are good for eating cactuses. These finches will be better at getting food—they're better adapted to their environment—so they are more likely to survive and have young…"

"They'll have more young than the other finches. So then, more finch chicks will be born with beaks that are good for eating cactuses," said Lucía, starting to get it.

"That's right," said Darwin. "The helpful changes get

passed on to the next generation. At the same time, finches with poorly adapted beaks will be less likely to survive and reproduce. If you imagine this happening over millions of years, generation after generation, you can understand how each island eventually produces finches with such well-adapted beaks."

"It's a great theory!" said Ning.

"Thank you," said Darwin. "I call it *evolution by natural selection.*"

"And it has to take generations, does it?" asked Marcus. "It couldn't happen, for example, that an animal suddenly evolves into something else?"

"No, that's not the way it happens," said Darwin. "And a good thing, too, if you ask me. You wouldn't want your dog suddenly to turn into a cat, would you?"

Orbit let out a horrified whine.

"No, that would be terrible," said Marcus, "especially for him!"

Chapter 7

Bones of the Past

Back at Zac's house, the children decided it was time for some lunch.

"So, what have we learned so far?" asked Zac, as he made sandwiches for his friends.

"We know that the mystery beast probably isn't from around here," said Lucía. "It's most likely an invader."

"And, it's almost certainly a species that's already been discovered," added Ning.

"And, it's probably not newly evolved," sighed Marcus. "Like other species, it's a product of generations of evolution."

"Very good," said Zac. "It sounds like we're getting somewhere. Any other ideas about what kind of creature it might be?"

"I'd say it's probably pretty rare," said Ning. "It may even be the last of its kind."

"I don't believe that," said Marcus. "The mystery beast has to be big, brave, and strong. Otherwise, it wouldn't go around raiding people's backyards every night. A species like that wouldn't just die off."

"I wouldn't be so sure," said Zac. "Did you know that around 99 percent of all species that have ever lived on Earth are now extinct? That means they've died off completely. And, many of them were big, brave, and strong."

Marcus looked puzzled. "But Darwin told us that the best adapted animals were more likely to survive. For sure it's a good adaptation to be big, brave, and strong."

"Not necessarily," said Zac. "What Darwin actually said is that the animals best adapted to their environment were most likely to survive. If your environment changes and you can't adapt, it doesn't matter how big, brave, and strong you are—you're doomed! Think of the dinosaurs. Many of them had evolved into huge, powerful beasts by the time they died out around 65 million years ago."

"What happened to them?" asked Lucía.

"Most scientists believe they were wiped out by a giant asteroid strike or volcanic eruptions," replied Zac. "These disasters would have caused big changes to Earth's atmosphere and climate, and the dinosaurs couldn't handle it."

"It's sad when you think about all the millions of species we'll never get to see because they died out before we came along," said Ning.

"You're not alone in feeling that way," said Zac.

"Not long ago, most people didn't think it was even possible for an animal to go extinct. The first person to suggest that a species could die out was a Frenchman, Georges Cuvier—pronounced *zhawrzh KOOV yay*—in 1796. He was a pioneer of paleontology—the study of fossils. If you want to, we can go and meet him after we finish lunch."

The friends all agreed that would be a good idea. So, half an hour later, there was another flash and a zoom. They arrived in a gloomy, old-fashioned laboratory in the late 1700's. The shelves were lined with books and with trays that held animal bones. Mounted on a stand in the middle of the room was a large fossil—the bones of a prehistoric animal that had been preserved in stone. A man in a long coat was studying it by the light of a flickering candle. With its long, curving tusks, the fossil looked like the skull of an elephant.

"That's Georges Cuvier," whispered Zac. "The man, I mean—not the fossil!"

Just then, Orbit found a bone on one of the lower

shelves. He jumped up on his hind legs and snatched it in his jaws. Zac tried to grab it, but Orbit didn't want to let go. A noisy struggle followed.

Cuvier spun around. "What is going on?" he asked. Then, he gasped, "*Quelle horreur!* What horror! That bone is over a thousand years old! Get it away from your dog!"

Zac finally yanked the bone from Orbit's mouth. He wiped it clean of slobber and returned it to the shelf. "I'm so sorry, monsieur!"

"What is the meaning of this disturbance?" demanded Cuvier.

"We wanted to ask you about extinction, monsieur," Zac said.

"Extinction, eh!" growled Cuvier. "Now that might be a fitting fate for that mutt of yours!" He said this, though, with a twinkle in his eye. Zac was relieved to see that the paleontologist was no longer angry.

"I am joking, of course!" said Cuvier. "Actually, it pleases me greatly that you are interested in this new theory of mine. So far, I have had nothing but insults from everyone I speak to about extinction."

"Sometimes people don't want to hear the truth," said Marcus.

"You are absolutely right, young man," Cuvier

said, nodding. "But maybe they will now, for I have recently found strong evidence to support my theory."

"What have you discovered?" asked Ning.

Cuvier pointed to the skull he'd been examining. "This fossil," he said, "was dug up in Ohio country, in the United States. It looks like the skull of an elephant, right?"

They all nodded.

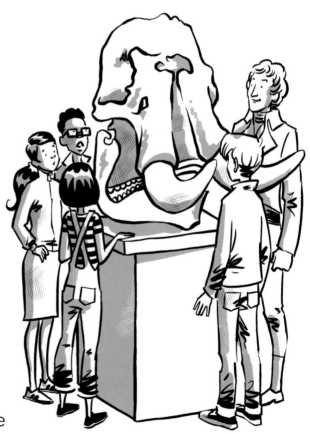

"Wrong!" declared Cuvier. "The lower jaw differs from that of any living elephant. This is a species of elephant that no longer exists. It is extinct. Of course, my fellow scholars will not like this idea. They will say, 'But, Monsieur Cuvier, it must exist somewhere on Earth, we just haven't found it yet.' Nonsense! How can such an enormous animal go undiscovered for so long?"

"How do you think it went extinct?" asked Lucía.

"There was a great catastrophe," Cuvier answered firmly. "Evidence of it can be found in ancient rocks, if you know what to look for. There was a terrible flood that led to the extinction of huge numbers of species. This explains the strange fossils that people have been digging up lately—the remains of giant lizards that do not walk among us today."

Ning whispered to Zac, "I think he's talking about dinosaurs."

Zac nodded, and whispered back, "Yes, but that word wasn't invented until 1842." He turned to Cuvier. "Thank you for sharing your theory with us, monsieur. We wish you luck in convincing others of your views."

"You are most welcome, my friends. Au revoir!"

Cuvier turned his attention back to the fossil, and Zac pressed a button on his phone. A moment later, the children were back in Zac's kitchen.

"Hooray for Cuvier for being the first to realize extinction is a thing," said Marcus. "It can't be easy being right when everyone around you thinks you're wrong. Boy, do I know how that feels!"

"Sure," said Zac, "although Cuvier wasn't right about everything. He believed animals could only go extinct during big catastrophes. In fact, species die out all the time. They can be endangered by changes to their environment or threats from diseases or predators. Today, things that human beings do—like polluting and destroying habitat—are pushing many species toward extinction."

Chapter 8

A Breakthrough

The next day, the children were in the mood for some real-world investigation. Lucía suggested they check Zac's yard again. "We could take a closer look around the fence, where we saw the mystery beast," she said. "Maybe we missed something."

This time, they searched the ground and the trampled plants even more carefully. Unfortunately, the ground was dry, so the creature had left no footprints. They examined the broken flower stems, hoping to find a trace of fur or some other evidence, but there was nothing. They analyzed the scratches on the fence. Ning noticed that they were broad and not too deep. She figured that the claws that had made them—if they were claws—were wide and blunt, not sharp like the claws of a cat.

While they were studying these marks, Orbit began to bark. The children all turned to see him nosing around among some bushes against the fence.

"What is it, boy?" said Zac. He squatted down and peered through the leaves that Orbit had been sniffing. "There's a hole in the fence," Zac called out. "We didn't see it before because it's behind these bushes."

Zac showed the others how the branches were bent, as if something had barged through them. "I think the mystery beast may have come into the yard through here," he concluded.

"What's on the other side of this fence?" asked Ning.

"It's just some brush along the side of a creek, which eventually leads to the forest preserve," said Zac.

Suddenly, Orbit broke free of Zac's grip. He crashed through the bush and wriggled through the hole.

"I think he smells something!" said Lucía. "Let's follow him."

One at a time, the children pushed their way through the bushes and squeezed through the hole in the fence.

They came out on the other side in a patch of waist-high grass. Orbit barked excitedly, scampering around a patch of mud near the fence. Planted in the mud was a footprint.

"Hey, it's just like the footprint I found in the forest preserve!" cried Ning. "See how the big toe sticks out from the rest of the foot." She found the picture she had taken her phone and showed it to them. The two prints were an exact match.

"You're right!" said Zac. "It must belong to our mystery beast." He hugged Orbit. "Well done, boy! This is a real breakthrough."

"Woof!" barked Orbit proudly. He wagged his tail.

"This is great!" said Marcus. "Now all we need to figure out is what kind of animal makes a footprint like that."

"Come and look at this, everyone!" Lucía called suddenly. She was crouching by the hole in the fence. On one side of the hole, a nail stuck out of a fence post. Something had snagged on it.

Zac squinted at it. Then, very carefully, he picked it off the nail and laid it in his palm. It was a little tuft of black fur.

"It's definitely not Orbit's fur," said Zac.

"Then it has to belong to the mystery beast," said Lucía. "It must have caught on the nail when the beast was crawling through the hole."

"Well-spotted, Lu!" said Ning. "So now we have a footprint and some fur."

"We may have something else, too," said Zac. He pointed out a tiny white dot at one end of a single hair. "This," he said, "is the hair follicle. It's the skin cells that surround the root of the hair."

"Why is that important?" asked Marcus.

"Because it contains DNA," replied Zac.

"What's DNA?" asked Lucía.

"DNA is the material in a living cell that carries the genes," Zac explained.

Ning frowned as she tried to remember what the wildlife scientist had told them about genes. "Genes," she recalled, "are the part of an animal's cells that determine which traits the animal inherits from its parents."

"That's right," said Zac. "And by examining its genes, we can find out what species of animal it is. In fact, let's take a look at the DNA now, using the microscope app I've been working on."

He pressed a button on his phone and held it over the follicle. The others gathered around to look at the screen. Zac dragged a finger across the screen, and the follicle grew bigger and bigger. Soon, they could see the individual cells on its surface. As he continued to zoom in, they could see inside one of the cells.

Zac pointed out a ball in the cell's middle. "That's the nucleus, the part of the cell where the DNA is," he explained.

The view on the screen continued to enlarge until it showed the inside of the nucleus. Floating within were strange things like tangled bits of string. They looked a little like stretched out letter X's.

"Those things are called chromosomes," explained Zac, "and they contain the DNA."

He zoomed in on one of the chromosomes, and they saw it was made up of an extremely long, coiled strand. It looked like an endless twisting ladder with countless rungs.

"That spiraling thing that looks like a ladder is the DNA," said Zac. "The rungs are made up of chemicals called bases. There are four bases altogether. The order of the bases makes up a code—the code in which the genes are written."

"How's that going to help us," asked Marcus. "I don't know how to read gene code."

"Neither do I," said Zac. "But each kind of animal has different genes, and so a different code. So, by comparing this to DNA samples taken from known animals, I should be able to identify our mystery beast."

Chapter 9
The Mystery Beast

Back at the house, Zac went up to his room. He planned to use his laboratory equipment to compare the DNA to samples from other animals.

The others hung around in the kitchen, with nothing to do but wait for Zac to solve the mystery. They were soon bored.

Orbit whined and padded restlessly by the kitchen door.

"Poor thing wants to go out," said Marcus.

"I know how he feels!" said Lucía. "But it doesn't seem right leaving Zac to do all the work while we go outside and play. I wish we could help him."

"Maybe we can," said Ning. "How about we try to lure the mystery beast into Zac's yard by laying a trail of food for it."

"What kind of food?" asked Lucía.

"Well, it tore up Miss Sanchez's vegetable patch, so it obviously likes vegetables," said Ning.

"A vegetarian mystery beast," chuckled Marcus. "Somehow that sounds a little less scary!"

The three of them rode their bikes to the grocery store. Putting together their pocket change, they bought carrots, zucchini, potatoes, and cabbages.

Back at the house, they went upstairs and asked Zac how his search was going.

"No match yet," he muttered, lost in his work.

Lucía, Ning, and Marcus returned to the kitchen. With some help from Zac's dad, they chopped up the vegetables.

When they had filled three bags, they took Orbit into the yard and pushed their way through the hole in the fence. They fought through the dense grass until they came to an old path that ran along the creek. The path led them to the forest preserve.

The three children began laying a trail of food from the edge of the forest preserve back toward Zac's house. The trail ended in the middle of the back yard, where they piled the remaining vegetables.

Back in the kitchen, they pulled up chairs by the rear window and began their lookout.

An hour later, the sky outside began to darken. Zac sat back in his chair, blinking. He must be mistaken—his eyes were tired after staring at his computer screen for so long— but it looked like he had found a match for the mystery DNA. Yet, no matter how he thought about it, it didn't seem possible. He decided to double-check…

Downstairs, in the kitchen, Ning, Lucía, and Marcus kept their watch over the yard. It was getting darker by the minute.

Suddenly, Orbit began to whine. He scampered over to the back door and gave a low, nervous bark.

Marcus leaned forward and squinted through the gloom toward the rear of the yard. "Something's coming," he hissed. "See how the bushes are moving?"

"You're right!" whispered Lucía.

Ning, Marcus, and Lucía leaped out of their chairs as the animal came into view…

"It has to be a match," Zac murmured to himself, staring at the DNA sequence on the screen. He got up, rushed out of his room, and charged down the stairs. "I've solved it!" he cried, barging into the kitchen. "I know what the mystery beast is!"

To Zac's surprise, none of them—not even Orbit—paid him any attention. Their eyes were locked on whatever they were staring at outside the window.

"Hey!" Zac cried. "The mystery beast is ..."

"A chimpanzee!" shouted Ning, Lucía, and Marcus together.

"How did you know?" gasped Zac. He followed their gaze, and there it was—a large chimpanzee. It was sitting in the middle of the lawn, chomping happily on a pile of vegetables.

Zac ran to get his father, and together they called the police. The woman who answered told them that no one should go near the animal. She said a police officer would be over soon, together with a trained animal handler.

Zac rejoined the others to keep watch on the chimp. It seemed content sitting there, chewing on carrots and zucchini. Unfortunately, it soon turned to snacking on

some of Zac's dad's prized flowers.

"A chimpanzee!" Marcus marveled. "I thought they lived in Africa. How is this possible?"

The answer to Marcus's question came soon. That's when the police officer showed up, along with a zookeeper from the local zoo.

The zookeeper was relieved to see the chimpanzee. His name, she told them, was Gombe. He had escaped his habitat at the zoo five days earlier.

The police officer crept around behind the fence, hoping to block Gombe's escape. Keeping a careful eye on the chimpanzee, the zookeeper brought a large crate into Zac's backyard. She opened the crate and tried gently to coax Gombe inside. The chimp seemed to recognize her, but he kept a cautious distance.

Suddenly, the zookeeper had a thought. She reached into her bag and pulled out a raggedy, chewed up old teddy bear. Gombe's eyes lit up. He wobbled over to her, stretching out his arms.

The zookeeper handed Gombe the teddy bear and prodded him into the crate. Gombe looked suddenly tired from his adventures. He hugged the teddy bear and snuggled into the corner of the crate.

With the crate safely in her van, the zookeeper returned to the house. "I want to thank you kids for helping us find him," she said. "As a reward, here are free tickets to the zoo."

"That's fantastic! Thank you!" cried Ning.

The next day, the children visited the zoo. They saw a leopard lounging in a tree and a mother rhino with her baby. They laughed at the sight of seals leaping and catching fish tossed to them. They shuddered at the giant beetles in the insect house. But the best moment came when they watched Gombe being reunited with his friends in the chimpanzee habitat.

The other chimps bounded up to him. One placed its arms around Gombe, while the rest leaped about and shrieked with excitement. At first, Gombe seemed a bit overwhelmed. But it didn't take him long to recover his spirits. Soon, he was clambering around on the rocks and the wooden climbing frame and chewing on a tasty plant root.

"He looks happy to be home," remarked Zac.

"He's back with his friends," grinned Marcus.

"Nothing beats that, right?"

"Right!" agreed Lucía. "And getting regular meals again can't hurt, either."

"Oh, look, that other chimp's grooming him," said Ning. Gombe sat looking very relaxed as another chimp picked fleas from his fur. "I bet he missed that when he was living in the forest preserve!" she added.

"I wonder if he'll tell them about his adventures," said Marcus.

Suddenly, Gombe looked up. He'd noticed the children watching him. He stared back at them for a long time, and they all thought they saw a spark of something in his eyes—maybe gratitude.

"He remembers us," murmured Lucía.

"Of course he does," said Zac.

"But it was dark when he came into your yard last night, Zac," said Ning. "And we kept the kitchen lights off on purpose. He couldn't have seen us."

"Oh, I think he knew who we were before then," said Zac. "Remember that day we spent in the forest preserve? Didn't you feel like you were being watched?"

Meet the Scientists

Aristotle

Aristotle (384–322 B.C.) was an ancient Greek philosopher and scientist. He wrote on many different subjects, including animals. He studied some 500 species of mammals, birds, and fishes in developing his animal classification system.

Carolus Linnaeus

Carolus Linnaeus (*lih NEE uhs*) (1707–1778) was a Swedish scientist who studied plants and animals. He invented the modern system of classifying living things. He journeyed around Sweden to find and classify plants and animals.

Charles Elton

Charles Sutherland Elton (1900–1991) was an English *zoologist* (animal scientist) and pioneer of *ecology*. Ecology is the study of how living things relate to one another and to their environment. He established important principles of ecology and studied invasive species.

Charles Darwin

Charles Darwin (1809–1882) was an English naturalist and biologist. He developed the theory of evolution by natural selection, which he described in his book *On the Origin of Species* (1859). The principles of this theory are fundamental to the modern life sciences.

Georges Cuvier

Georges Cuvier (*zhawrzh koov YAY*) (1769–1832) was a French naturalist and zoologist. Cuvier compared living animals with fossils to try and prove that animals could go extinct—a controversial idea at the time. He believed there had been mass extinctions caused by catastrophes, such as floods, in Earth's past.

Glossary

adaptation a characteristic that helps a species survive in its environment

chromosome a threadlike structure in the cell nucleus that carries a living thing's DNA

diverse (in ecology) having many different kinds of species

DNA the material within chromosomes that carries *genetic* (hereditary) information, helping to determine a living thing's characteristics

ecosystem a community of living things along with their environment

evolution the process by which species develop over time

extinction when an entire kind of living thing dies off completely

fossil the remains or impression of a prehistoric animal embedded and preserved in rock

gene a sequence of DNA that corresponds to a particular trait, such as eye color

habitat destruction the damaging of an environment (for example, by farming, mining, logging, or overfishing) so that it can no longer support its native species

invertebrate an animal lacking a backbone, such as an insect, mollusk, or worm

mutation a change in the structure of a gene, resulting in a slightly different trait

natural selection the principle by which living things better suited to their environment survive and produce more offspring, spreading helpful traits

paleontology learning about living things through the study of fossils

predator a living thing that preys on, or eats, another

scientific classification the organization of living things into groups based on how they are related

selfie an informal self-portrait, usually taken with a cell phone

species a group of living things made up of individuals so similar that they can successfully breed with one another; a single kind of living thing

vertebrate an animal with a backbone, such as a mammal, bird, reptile, or fish

virtual created and existing only in a computer—like the historical scenes visited in Zac's Backspace app

Additional Resources

Books

Animal Classification (Life Science Stories)
Angela Royston (Raintree, 2017)

Early Life on Earth (Planet Earth)
Michael Bright (Wayland, 2018)

Evolution (Raintree Perspectives: Great Scientific Theories)
Nick Hunter (Raintree, 2017)

Woodland Forest Ecosystems (Ecosystems of the World)
Racquel Foran (Core Library, 2015)

Websites

Active Wild – Animal Classification

https://www.activewild.com/animal-classification/

A simple, clear explanation of how scientists go about identifying and naming animal species and organizing them into groups

Discover Wildlife (BBC Wildlife Magazine) – Evolution: First Life

http://www.discoverwildlife.com/animals/evolution-first-life

Learn about some of the animals at the roots of the tree of life: the first land animal, the first to have a head and a tail, etc.

National Geographic – Invasive Species

https://www.nationalgeographic.org/encyclopedia/invasive-species/

This website explains what invasive species are, how they are introduced to an ecosystem, the harm they can do, and what we can do to remove them.

Index